Book 1
C Programming Professional Made Easy

BY SAM KEY

&

Book 2
CSS Programming Professional Made Easy

BY SAM KEY

Book 1
C Programming Professional Made Easy

BY SAM KEY

Expert C Programming Language Success In A Day For Any Computer User!

Programming Box Set #29: C Programming Professional Made Easy & CSS Programming Professional Made Easy

Programming Box Set #29: C Programming Professional Made Easy & CSS Programming Professional Made Easy

Table Of Contents

Introduction

I want to thank you and congratulate you for purchasing the book, “Professional C Programming Made Easy: Expert C Programming Language Success In A Day For Any Computer User!”.

This book contains proven steps and strategies on how to understand and perform C programming. C is one of the most basic programming tools used for a wide array of applications. Most people stay away from it because the language seem complicated, with all those characters, letters, sequences and special symbols.

This book will break down every element and explain in detail each language used in the C program. By the time you are done with this book, C programming language will be easy to understand and easy to execute.

Read on and learn.

Thanks again for purchasing this book. I hope you enjoy it!

Chapter 1 The Basic Elements Of C

The seemingly complicated C program is composed of the following basic elements:

Character Set

The alphabet in both upper and lower cases is used in C. The 0-9 digits are also used, including white spaces and some special characters. These are used in different combinations to form elements of a basic C program such as expressions, constants, variables, etc.

Special characters include the following:

+ ,. *– / % = & ! #?”^ ‘| / ( )< > { } [ ] ;: @ ~!

White spaces include:

- Blank space
- Carriage return
- Horizontal tab
- Form feed
- New line

Identifiers

An identifier is a name given to the various elements of the C program, such as arrays, variables and functions. These contain digits and letters in various arrangements. However, identifiers should always start with a letter. The letters may be in upper case, lower case or both. However, these are not interchangeable. C programming is case sensitive, as each letter in different cases is regarded as separate from each other. Underscores are also permitted because it is considered by the program as a kind of letter.

Examples of valid identifiers include the following:

ab123

A

stud_name

average

velocity

TOTAL

Identifiers need to start with a letter and should not contain illegal characters. Examples of invalid identifiers include the following:

2nd	- should always start with a letter
"Jamshedpur"	- contains the illegal character (")
stud name	- contains a blank space, which is an illegal character
stud-name	- contains an illegal character (-)

In C, a single identifier may be used to refer to a number of different entities within the same C program. For instance, an array and a variable can share one identifier. For example:

The variable is int difference, average, A[5]; // sum, average

The identifier is A[5].

In the same program, an array can be named A, too.

__func__

The __func__ is a predefined identifier that provides functions names and makes these accessible and ready for use anytime in the function. The complier would automatically declare the __func__ immediately after placing the opening brace when declaring the function definitions. The compiler declares the predefined identifier this way:

static const char _ _func_ _[] = "Alex";

"Alex" refers to a specific name of this particular function.

Take a look at this example:

```
#include <stdio.h>


void anna1(void)   {
      printf("%sn",__func__);
      return;
}


int main() {
    myfunc();
}
```

What will appear as an output will be anna1

Keywords

Reserved words in C that come with standard and predefined meanings are called keywords. The uses for these words are restricted to their predefined intended purpose. Keywords cannot be utilized as programmer-defined identifiers. In C, there are 32 keywords being used, which include the following:

auto	default
break	double
char	float
case	else
continue	extern
const	enum
do	goto

for	switch
if	typedef
long	struct
int	union
register	switch
short	void
return	unsigned
sizeof	while
signed	volatile

Data Types

There are different types of data values that are passed in C. Each of the types of data has different representations within the memory bank of the computer. These also have varying memory requirements. Data type modifiers/qualifiers are often used to augment the different types of data.

Supported data types in C include int, char, float, double, void, _Bool, _Complex, arrays, and constants.

int

Integer quantities are stored in this type of data. The data type *int* can store a collection of different values, starting from INT_MAX to INT_MIN. An in-header file, <limits h>, defines the range.

These int data types use type modifiers such as unsigned, signed, long, long long and short.

Short int means that they occupy memory space of only 2 bytes.

A long int uses 4 bytes of memory space.

Short unsigned int is a data type that uses 2 bytes of memory space and store positive values only, ranging from 0 to 65535.

Unsigned int requires memory space similar to that of short unsigned int. For regular and ordinary int, the bit at the leftmost portion is used for the integer's sign.

Long unsigned int uses 4 bytes of space. It stores all positive integers ranging from 0 to 4294967295.

An int data is automatically considered as signed.

Long long int data type uses 64 bits memory. This type may either be unsigned or signed. Signed long long data type can store values ranging from —9,223,372,036,854,775,808 to 9,223,372,036,854,775,807. Unsigned long long data type stores value range of 0 to 18,446,744,073,709,551,615.

char

Single characters such as those found in C program's character set are stored by this type of data. The char data type uses 1 byte in the computer's memory. Any value from C program's character set can be stored as char. Modifiers that can be used are either unsigned or signed.

A char would always use 1 byte in the computer's memory space, whether it is signed or unsigned. The difference is on the value range. Values that can be stored as unsigned char range from 0 to 255. Signed char stores values ranging from —128 to +127. By default, a char data type is considered unsigned.

For each of the char types, there is a corresponding integer interpretation. This makes each char a special short integer.

float

A float is a data type used in storing real numbers that have single precision. That is, precision denoted as having 6 more digits after a decimal point. Float data type uses 4 bytes memory space.

The modifier for this data type is long, which uses the same memory space as that of double data type.

double

The double data type is used for storing real numbers that have double precision. Memory space used is 8 bytes. Double data type uses long as a type modifier. This uses up memory storage space of 10 bytes.

void

Void data type is used for specifying empty sets, which do not contain any value. Hence, void data type also occupies no space (0 bytes) in the memory storage.

_Bool

This is a Boolean type of data. It is an unsigned type of integer. It stores only 2 values, which is 0 and 1. When using _Bool, include **<stdboolh>**.

_Complex

This is used for storing complex numbers. In C, three types of _Complex are used. There is the float _Complex, double _Complex, and long double _Complex. These are found in <complex h> file.

Arrays

This identifier is used in referring to the collection of data that share the same name and of the same type of data. For example, all integers or all characters that have the same name. Each of the data is represented by its own array element. The subscripts differentiate the arrays from each other.

Constants

Constants are identifiers used in C. The values of identifiers do not change anywhere within the program. Constants are declared this way:

```
const datatype varname = value
```

const is the keyword that denotes or declares the variable as the fixed value entity, i.e., the constant.

In C, there are 4 basic constants used. These include the integer constant, floating-point, character and string constants. Floating-point and integer types of constant do not contain any blank spaces or commas. Minus signs can be used, which denotes negative quantities.

Integer Constants

Integer constants are integer valued numbers consisting of sequence of digits. These can be written using 3 different number systems, namely, decimal, octal and hexadecimal.

Decimal system (base 10)

An integer constant written in the decimal system contains combinations of numbers ranging from 0 to 9. Decimal constants should start with any number other except 0. For example, a decimal constant is written in C as:

```
const int size =76
```

Octal (base 8)

Octal constants are any number combinations from 0 to 7. To identify octal constants, the first number should be 0. For example:

```
const int a= 043; const int b=0;
```

An octal constant is denoted in the binary form. Take the octal 0347. Each digit is represented as:

$$0347 = 011\ 100\ 111 = 3 * 8^2 + 4 * 8^1 + 7 * 8^0 = 231$$

```
--- --- ---
 3   4   7
```

Hexadecimal constant (base 16)

This type consists of any of the possible combinations of digits ranging from 0 to 9. This type also includes letters a to f, written in either lowercase or uppercase. To identify hexadecimal constants, these should start with oX or oX. For example:

```
const int c= 0x7FF;
```

For example, the hexadecimal number 0x2A5 is internally represented in bit patterns within C as:

$$0x2A5 = 0010\ 1010\ 0101 = 2 * 16^2 + 10 * 16^1 + 5 * 16^0 = 677$$

```
---- ---- ----
  2    A    5
```

Wherein, 677 is the decimal equivalent of the hexadecimal number 0x2.

Prefixes for integer constants can either be long or unsigned. A long integer constant (long int) ends with a l of L, such as 67354L or 67354l. The last portion of an unsigned long integer constant should either be ul or UL, such as 672893UL or 672893ul. For an unsigned long long integer constant, UL or ul should be at the last portion. An unsigned constant should end with U or u, such as 673400095u or 673400095U. Normal integer constants are written without any suffix, such as a simple 67458.

Floating Point Constant

This type of constant has a base 10 or base 16 and contains an exponent, a decimal point or both. For a floating point constant with a base 10 and a decimal point, the base is replaced by an E or e. For example, the constant 1.8 *10^-3 is written as 1.8e-3 or 1.8E-3.

For hexadecimal character constants and the exponent is in the binary form, the exponent is replaced by P or p. Take a look at this example:

This type of constant is often precision quantities. These occupy around 8 bytes of memory. Different add-ons are allowed in some C program versions, such as F for a single precision floating constant or L for a long floating point type of constant.

Character Constant

A sequence of characters, whether single or multiple ones, enclosed by apostrophes or single quotation marks is called a character constant. The character set in the computer determines the integer value equivalent to each character constant. Escape sequences may also be found within the sequence of a character constant.

Single character constants enclosed by apostrophes is internally considered as integers. For example, ‘A’ is a single character constant that has an integer value of 65. The corresponding integer value is also called the ASCII value. Because of the corresponding numerical value, single character constants can be used in calculations just like how integers are used. Also, these constants can also be used when comparing other types of character constants.

Prefixes used in character constants such as L, U or u are used for character literals. These are considered as wide types of character constants. Character literals with the prefix L are considered under the type wchar_t, which are defined as <stddef.h> under the header file. Character constants that use the prefix U or u are considered as type char16_t or char32_t. These are considered as unsigned types of characters and are defined under the header file as <uchar.h>.

Those that do not have the prefix L are considered a narrow or ordinary character constant. Those that have escape sequences or are composed of at least 2 characters are considered as multicharacter constants.

Escape sequences are a type of character constant used in expressing non-printing characters like carriage return or tab. This sequence always begins with a backward slash, followed by special characters. These sequences represent a single character in the C language even if they are composed of more than 1 character. Examples of some of the most common escape sequences, and their integer (ASCII) value, used in C include the following:

Character	**Escape Sequence**	**ASCII Value**
Backspace	\b	008
Bell	\a	007
Newline	\n	010
Null	\o	000
Carriage	\r	013
Horizontal tab	\t	009
Vertical tab	\v	011
Form feed	\f	012

String Literals

Multibyte characters that form a sequence are called string literals. Multibyte characters have bit representations that fit into 1 or more bytes. String literals are enclosed within double quotation marks, for example, "A" and "Anna". There are 2 types of string literals, namely, UTF-8 string literals and wide string literals. Prefixes used for wide string literals include u, U or L. Prefix for UTF-8 string literals is u8.

Additional characters or extended character sets included in string literals are recognized and supported by the compiler. These additional characters can be used meaningfully to further enhance character constants and string literals.

Symbolic constants

Symbolic constants are substitute names for numeric, string or character constants within a program. The compiler would replace the symbolic constants with its actual value once the program is run.

At the beginning of the program, the symbolic constant is defined with a # **define** feature. This feature is called the preprocessor directive.

The definition of a symbolic constant does not end with a semi colon, like other C statements. Take a look at this example:

```
#define PI 3.1415
```

(//PI is the constant that will represent value 3.1415)

```
#define True 1

#define name "Alice"
```

For all numeric constants such as floating point and integer, non-numeric characters and blank spaces are not included. These constants are also limited by minimum and maximum bounds, which are usually dependent on the computer.

Variables

Memory locations where data is stored are called variables. These are indicated by a unique identifier. Names for variables are symbolic representations that refer to a particular memory location. Examples are *count, car_no* and *sum.*

Rules when writing the variable names

Writing variable names follow certain rules in order to make sure that data is stored properly and retrieved efficiently.

- Letters (in both lowercase and uppercase), underscore ('_') and digits are the only characters that can be used for variable names.

- Variables should begin either with an underscore or a letter. Starting with an underscore is acceptable, but is not highly recommended. Underscores at the beginning of variables can come in conflict with system names and the compiler may protest.

- There is no limit on the length of variables. The compiler can distinguish the first 31 characters of a variable. This means that individual variables should have different sequences for the 1st 31 characters.

Variables should also be declared at the beginning of a program before it can be used.

Chapter 2 What is C Programming Language?

In C, the programming language is a language that focuses on the structure. It was developed in 1972, at Bell Laboratories, by Dennis Ritchie. The features of the language were derived from “B”, which is an earlier programming language and formally known as BCPL or Basic Combined Programming Language. The C programming language was originally developed to implement the UNIX operating system.

Standards of C Programming Language

In 1989, the American National Standards Institute developed the 1st standard specifications. This pioneering standard specification was referred to as C89 and C90, both referring to the same programming language.

In 1999, a revision was made in the programming language. The revised standard was called C99. It had new features such as advanced data types. It also had a few changes, which gave rise to more applications.

The C11 standard was developed, which added new features to the programming language for C. This had a library-like generic macro type, enhanced Unicode support, anonymous structures, multi-threading, bounds-checked functions and atomic structures. It had improved compatibility with C++. Some parts of the C99 library in C11 were made optional.

The Embedded C programming language included a few features that were not part of C. These included the named address spaces, basic I/O hardware addressing and fixed point arithmetic.

C Programming Language Features

There are a lot of features of the programming language, which include the following:

- Modularity
- Interactivity
- Portability
- Reliability

- Effectiveness
- Efficiency
- Flexibility

Uses of the C Programming Language

This language has found several applications. It is now used for the development of system applications, which form a huge portion of operating systems such as Linux, Windows and UNIX.

Some of the applications of C language include the following:

- Spreadsheets
- Database systems
- Word processors
- Graphics packages
- Network drivers
- Compilers and Assemblers
- Operating system development
- Interpreters

Chapter 3 Understanding C Program

The C program has several features and steps in order for an output or function is carried out.

Basic Commands (for writing basic C Program)

The basic syntax and commands used in writing a simple C program include the following:

```
#include <stdio.h>
```

This command is a preprocessor. <stdio.h> stands for standard input output header file. This is a file from the C library, which is included before the C program is compiled.

```
int main()
```

Execution of all C program begins with this main function.

```
{
```

This symbol is used to indicate the start of the main function.

```
}
```

This indicates the conclusion of the main function.

```
/* */
```

Anything written in between this command will not be considered for execution and compilation.

```
printf (output);
```

The printf command prints the output on the screen.

```
getch();
```

Writing this command would allow the system to wait for any keyboard character input.

```
return 0
```

Writing this command will terminate the C program or main function and return to 0.

A basic C Program would look like this:

```
#include <stdio.h>
int main()
{
/* Our first simple C basic program */
printf("Hello People! ");
getch();
return 0;
}
```

The output of this simple program would look like this:

```
Hello People!
```

Chapter 4 Learn C Programming

After learning the basic elements and what the language is all about, time to start programming in C. Here are the most important steps:

Download a compiler

A compiler is a program needed to compile the C code. It interprets the written codes and translates it into specific signals, which can be understood by the computer. Usually, compiler programs are free. There are different compilers available for several operating systems. Microsoft Visual Studio and MinGW are compilers available for Windows operating systems. XCode is among the best compilers for Mac. Among the most widely used C compiler options for Linux is gcc.

Basic Codes

Consider the following example of a simple C program in the previous chapter:

```
#include <stdio.h>


int main()

{

  printf("Hello People!\n");

  getchar();

  return 0;

}
```

At the start of the program, #include command is placed. This is important in order to load the libraries where the needed functions are located.

The <stdio.h> refers to the file library and allows for the use of the succeeding functions getchar() and printf().

The command int main () sends a message to the compiler to run the function with the name "main" and return a certain integer once it is done running. Every C program executes a main function.

The symbol { } is used to specify that everything within it is a component of the "main" function that the compiler should run.

The function printf() tells the system to display the words or characters within the parenthesis onto the computer screen. The quotation marks make certain that the C compiler would print the words or characters as it is. The sequence \n informs the C compiler to place its cursor to the succeeding line. At the conclusion of the line, a ; (semicolon) is placed to denote that the sequence is done. Most codes in C program needs a semicolon to denote where the line ends.

The command getchar() informs the compiler to stop once it reaches the end of the function and standby for an input from the keyboard before continuing. This command is very useful because most compilers would run the C program and then immediately exits the window. The getchar() command would prevent the compiler to close the window until after a keystroke .is made.

The command return 0 denotes that the function has ended. For this particular C program, it started as an int, which indicates that the program has to return an integer once it is done running. The "0" is an indication that the compiler ran the program correctly. If another number is returned at the end of the program, it means that there was an error somewhere in the program.

Compiling the program

To compile the program, type the code into the program's code editor. Save this as a type of *.c file, then click the Run or Build button.

Commenting on the code

Any comments placed on codes are not compiled. These allow the user to give details on what happens in the function. Comments are good reminders on what the code is all about and for what. Comments also help other developers to understand what the code when they look at it.

To make a comment, add a /* at the beginning of the comment. End the written comment with a */. When commenting, comment on everything except the basic portions of the code, where explanations are no longer necessary because the meanings are already clearly understood.

Also, comments can be utilized for quick removal of code parts without having to delete them. Just enclose portions of the code in /* */, then compile. Remove these tags if these portions are to be added back into the code.

USING VARIABLES

Understanding variables

Define the variables before using them. Some common ones include char, float and int.

Declaring variables

Again, variables have to be declared before the program can use them. To declare, enter data type and then the name of the variable. Take a look at these examples:

```
char name;

float x;

int f, g, i, j;
```

Multiple variables can also be declared all on a single line, on condition that all of them belong to the same data type. Just separate the names of the variables commas (i.e., int f, g, i, j;).

When declaring variables, always end the line with a semicolon to denote that the line has ended.

Location on declaring the variables

Declaring variables is done at the start of the code block. This is the portion of the code enclosed by the brackets {}. The program won't function well if variables are declared later within the code block.

Variables for storing user input

Simple programs can be written using variables. These programs will store inputs of the user. Simple programs will use the function scanf, which searches the user's input for particular values. Take a look at this example:

```
#include <stdio.h>

int main()
{
 int x;

 printf( "45: " );
 scanf( "%d", &x );
 printf( "45 %d", x );
 getchar();
 return 0;
}
```

The string &d informs the function scanf to search the input for any integers.

The command & placed before the x variable informs the function scanf where it can search for the specific variable so that the function can change it. It also informs the function to store the defined integer within the variable.

The last printf tells the compiler to read back the integer input into the screen as a feedback for the user to check.

Manipulating variables

Mathematical expressions can be used, which allow users to manipulate stored variables. When using mathematical expressions, it is most important to remember to use the "=" distinction. A single = will set the variable's value. A == (double equal sign) is placed when the goal is to compare the values on both sides of the sign, to check if the values are equal.

For example:

```
x = 2 * 4; /* sets the value of "x" to 2 * 4, or 8 */
```

```
x = x + 8; /* adds 8 to the original "x " value, and defines the new "x" value as the specific variable */
```

```
x == 18; /* determines if the value of "x" is equal to 18 */
```

```
x < 11; /* determines if the "x" value is lower than 11 */
```

CONDITIONAL STATEMENTS

Conditional statements can also be used within the C program. In fact, most programs are driven by these statements. These are determined as either False or True and then acted upon depending on the results. The most widely used and basic conditional statement is if.

In C, False and True statements are treated differently. Statements that are "TRUE" are those that end up equal to nonzero numbers. For example, when a comparison is performed, the outcome is a "TRUE" statement if the returned numerical value is "1". The result is a "FALSE" statement if the value that returns is "0".

Basic conditional operators

The operation of conditional statements is based on mathematical operators used in comparing values. The most common conditional operators include the following:

```
<  /* less than */

6 < 15 TRUE

>  /* greater than */

10 > 5 TRUE

<=  /* less than or equal to */

4 <= 8 TRUE

>=  /* greater than or equal to */

8 >= 8 TRUE
```

```
!=  /* not equal to */

4 != 5 TRUE

==  /* equal to */

7 == 7 TRUE
```

How to write a basic "IF" conditional statement

A conditional "IF" statement is used in determining what the next step in the program is after evaluation of the statement. These can be combined with other types of conditional statements in order to create multiple and powerful options.

Take a look at this example:

```
#include <stdio.h>

int main()
{
 if ( 4 < 7 )
   printf( "4 is less than 7");
   getchar();
}
```

The "ELSE/ELSE IF" statements

These statements can be used in expanding the conditional statements. Build upon the "IF" statements with "ELSE" and "ELSE IF" type of conditional statements, which will handle different types of results. An "ELSE" statement will be run when the IF statement result is FALSE. An "ELSE IF" statement will allow for the inclusion of multiple IF statements in one code block, which will handle all the various cases of the statement.

Take a look at this example:

```
#include <stdio.h>

int main()
{
 int age;

 printf( "Please type current age: " );
 scanf( "%d", &age );
 if ( age <= 10 ) {
  printf( "You are just a kid!\n" );
 }
 else if ( age < 30 ) {
  printf( "Being a young adult is pretty awesome!\n" );
 }
 else if ( age < 50 ) {
  printf( "You are young at heart!\n" );
 }
 else {
  printf( "Age comes with wisdom.\n" );
 }
 return 0;
```

```
}
```

The above program will take all the input from the user and will run it through the different defined IF statements. If the input (number) satisfies the 1st IF statement, the 1st printf statement will be returned. If it does not, then input will be run through each of the "ELSE IF" statements until a match is found. If after all the "ELSE IF" statements have been run and nothing works, the input will be run through the "ELSE" statement at the last part of the program.

LOOPS

Loops are among the most important parts of C programming. These allow the user to repeat code blocks until particular conditions have been met. Loops make implementing repeated actions easy and reduce the need to write new conditional statements each time.

There are 3 main types of loops in C programming. These are FOR, WHILE and Do... WHILE.

"FOR" Loop

The "FOR" loop is the most useful and commonly used type of loop in C programming. This loop continues to run the function until the conditions set for this loop are met. There are 3 conditions required by the FOR loop. These include initialization of the variable, meeting the condition and how updating of the variable is done. All of these conditions need not be met at the same time, but a blank space with semicolon is still needed to prevent the loop from running continuously.

Take a look at this example:

```
#include <stdio.h>

int main()
{
 int y;

 for ( y = 0; y < 10; y++;){
```

```
printf( "%d\n", y );
}
getchar();
}
```

The value of *y* has been set to 0, and the loop is programmed to continue running as long as the *y* value remains less than 10. At each run (loop), the *y* value is increased by 1 before the loop is repeated. Hence, once the value of y is equivalent to 10 (after 10 loops), the above loop will then break.

WHILE Loop

These are simpler than the FOR loops. There is only one condition, which is that as long as the condition remains TRUE, the loop continues to run. Variables need not to be initialized or updated, but can be done within the loop's main body.

Take a look at this example:

```
#include <stdio.h>

int main()
{
int y;

while ( y <= 20 ){
printf( "%d\n", y );
y++;
}
```

```
getchar();

}
```

In the above program, the command y++ will add 1 to the variable *y* for each execution of the loop. When the value of *y* reaches 21, the loop will break.

DO...WHILE Loop

This is a very useful loop to ensure at least 1 run. FOR and WHILE loops check the conditions at the start of the loop, which ensures that it could not immediately pass and fail. DO...WHILE loops will check the conditions when the loop is finished. This ensures that the loop will run at last once before a pass and fail occurs.

Take a look at this example:

```
#include <stdio.h>

int main()

{

int y;

y = 10;

do {

printf("This loop is running!\n");

} while ( y != 10 );

getchar();

}
```

This type of loop displays the message whether the condition results turn out TRUE or FALSE. The *y* variable is set to 10. The WHILE loop has been set to run when the *y* value is not equal to 10, at which the loop ends. The message was printed because the condition is not checked until the loop has ended.

The WHILE portion of the DO..WHILE loop must end with a semicolon. This is also the only instance when a loop ends this way.

Conclusion

Thank you again for purchasing this book!

I hope this book was able to help you to understand the complex terms and language used in C. this programming method can put off a lot of users because of its seemingly complexity. However, with the right basic knowledge, soon, you will be programming more complex things with C.

The next step is to start executing these examples. Reading and understanding this book is not enough, although this will push you into the right direction. Execution will cement the knowledge and give you the skill and deeper understanding of C.

Finally, if you enjoyed this book, please take the time to share your thoughts and post a review on Amazon. We do our best to reach out to readers and provide the best value we can. Your positive review will help us achieve that. It'd be greatly appreciated!

Thank you and good luck!

Book 2
CSS Programming Professional Made Easy

BY SAM KEY

Expert CSS Programming Language Success in a Day for any Computer User!

Programming Box Set #29: C Programming Professional Made Easy & CSS Programming Professional Made Easy

Programming Box Set #29: C Programming Professional Made Easy & CSS Programming Professional Made Easy

Table of Contents

Introduction

I want to thank you and congratulate you for purchasing the book, "Professional CSS Programming Made Easy: Expert CSS Programming Language Success In A Day for any Computer User!".

This book contains proven steps and strategies on how to effectively apply CSS style rules in making your webpages more appealing to your readers. In this book, the different aspects of CSS programming are discussed in simple language to make it easy for you to understand even if you have no previous experience in programming. In no time, you can start creating your own CSS style rules!

Thanks again for purchasing this book, I hope you enjoy it!

Chapter 1: What is CSS?

CSS is short for Cascading Style Sheets which is a simple design language that is meant to streamline the enhancement of web page presentations. Basically, through CSS, you will be able to manage how a web page looks and feels. When you use CSS, you will be able to control the background color or image in the web page, the color of the texts, the style of the font, the size of the columns, the column layout, the spacing in between paragraphs and a whole lot more of design effects.

Even though CSS is quite simple to understand, it can provide you with great control of how an HTML document is presented. People who study CSS often study other markup languages such as XHTML or HTML.

What are the advantages of CSS?

- CSS will allow you to save time. After you have written a CSS code once, you can then use the same sheet in various web pages. You can create a style for each web page element and then use it to as many HTML pages as you desire in the future.
- Your web pages will load faster. If you will use CSS in your web pages, you no longer have to write an HTML tag attribute all the time. You simple create 1 CSS rule of a tag and then use it for all the incidences of that specific tag. When you use less HTML codes, it translates to faster download speed.
- Your web pages become easier to maintain. If you wish to create a global change in your website, all you need to do is adjust the style and then all the elements included in your different web pages will be automatically adjusted.
- You will be able to enjoy better styles compared to HTML. The style attributes available for HTML codes are lesser compared to what you can work with when you use CSS. This means that you will be able to create top quality styles for your web pages.
- You will have multiple device compatibility. With CSS, you will be allowed to use content that can be optimized for different types of device. Even when you use the same HTML document, you can present the website in various versions for different devices such as mobile phones, tablets, desktop and even printing.

- You will be able to adopt web standards that are recognized globally. More and more people are losing interest in using HTML attributes and have started to recommend the use of CSS.
- You get to future-proof. By using CSS in your web pages now, you can also ensure that they will have compatibility with future browsers.

Creation and Maintenance of CSS

Only a small group of people within the World Wide Web Consortium (W3C) referred to as the CSS Working Group is allowed to create and maintain CSS. This group generates the CSS specifications which are then submitted to the W3C members for discussion and ratification. Only ratified specifications are given the recommendation signal by the W3C. You need to note that they are referred to as recommendations since the W3C cannot really dictate how the language is to be actually implementation. The software the implement the CSS language is created by independent organizations and companies.

Note: If you wish to know, yes, the W3C is the group that provides the recommendations on how the Internet should work and how it should progress.

Different CSS Versions

The W3C released CSS1 or Cascading Style Sheets Level 1was released as a recommendation in 1996. The recommendation included a description of the CSS together with a basic visual formatting model that can be used for every HTML tag.

In May 1998, the W3C released the recommendation for CSS2 or Cascading Style Sheets Level 2 which included further information that builds on CSS1. CSS2 added support for style sheets for specific media such as aural devices, printers, element tables and positioning and downloadable fonts.

Chapter 2: Various Types of CSS Selectors

A CSS is composed of different style rules that are translated by the browser for them to be applied to the specific elements in your web page. A style rule is further composed of 3 parts: selector, property and value. A selector is the HTML tag wherein the style rule will be applied. Examples include <table> or <h1>. A property is the specific attribute type that an HTML tag has. In simple terms, you could say that each HTML attribute is ultimately translated to a CSS property. Examples of properties include border or color. Values, on the other hand, are directly assigned to the properties. For instance, for the color property, you can assign a value of #000000 or black.

One way to write a CSS Style Rule Syntax is: Selector (property: value)

Ex. You can write the syntax rule for a table border as: table (border: 2px solid #C00;). The selector in this example is table while the property is the border. The specific value given for the property is 2px solid #C00.

In this chapter, we will be talking about the different kinds of selectors.

Type Selector

The selector in the example given above (table) is categorized under the Type Selector. Another example of a type Selector is "level 1 heading" or "h1). We can write a CSS Style Rule Syntax as: h1 (color: #36CFFF;). The selector in this example is h1 while the property is the color. The specific value given for the property is #36CFFF.

Universal Selector

This is designated by an asterisk (*) which means that the style rule syntax that you want to create will be applied to all elements in your webpage and not only to specific elements.

Example: *(color: #FFFFFF;). This style rule means that you want all of the elements (including fonts, borders, etc.) in your webpage to be white.

Descendant Selector

You use the descendant selector when you wish to apply a certain style rule for a specific element that lies within a specific element.

Example: ul em (color:#FFFFFF;), the value #FFFFFF (white) will only be applied to the property (color) if the selector/property <em> lies within the selector <ul>.

Class Selector

Using the Class Selector, you will be able to define a specific style rule that can be applied based on the specific class attribute of elements. This means that all of the elements that have that specific class attributed will have the same formatting as specified in the style rule.

Example 1: .white (color: #FFFFFF;). Here the class attribute is "white" and it means that the color "white" will be applied to all of the elements given the class attribute "white" in your document.

Example 2: h1.white (color: #FFFFFF;). This style rule is more specific. The class attribute is still "white" and the style rule will be applied to the elements given the class attribute "white" but ONLY if they are ALSO an <h1> or "level 1 heading" element.

You can actually give one or more class selectors for each element. For example, you can give the class selectors "center" and "bold" to a paragraph <p> by writing it as <p class="center,bold">.

ID Selector

You use an ID selector to create a style rule that is based on the specific ID attribute of the element. This means that all of the elements that have that specific ID will have the same format as defined in the style rule.

Example 1: #white (color: #FFFFFF;). The ID assigned here is "white" and the style rule means that all elements with the "white" ID attribute will be rendered black in your document.

Example 2: h1#white (color: #FFFFFF;). This is more specific because it means that the style rule will only be applied to elements with the ID attribute "white" ONLY IF they are a level 1 heading element.

The ID selectors are ideally used as foundations for descendant selectors. Example: #white h3 (color: #FFFFFF;). The style rule dictates that all level 3 headings located in the different pages of your website will be displayed in white color ONLY IF those level 3 headings are within tags that have an ID attribute of "white".

Child Selector

The Child Selector is quite similar to the Descendant Selector except that they have different functionalities.

Example: body > p (color: #FFFFFF;). The style rule states that a paragraph will be rendered in white if it is a direct child of the <body> element. If the paragraph is within other elements such as <td> or <div>, the style rule will not apply to it.

Attribute Selector

You can apply specific styles to your webpage elements that have specific attributes.

Example: input(type="text"](color: #FFFFFF;).

One benefit of the above example is that the specified color in the style rule will only affect your desired text field and will not affect the <input type="submit"/>.

You need to keep the following rules in mind when using attribute selectors:

- p[lang]. All elements of the paragraph that has a "lang" attribute will be selected.

- p[lang="fr"]. All elements of the paragraph that has a "lang" attribute AND the value "fr" in the "lang" attribute will be selected. Note that the value should exactly be "fr".

- p[lang~="fr"]. All elements of the paragraph that has a "lang" attribute AND CONTAINS the value "fr" in the "lang" attribute will be selected.

- p[lang |="ne"]. All elements of the paragraph that has a "lang" attribute AND CONTAINS value that is EITHER exactly "en" or starts with "en-" in the "lang" attribute will be selected.

Multiple Style Rules

It is possible for you to create multiple style rules for one specific element. The style rules can be defined in such a way that different properties are combined into a single block and specific values are assigned to each property.

Example 1:

h1(color: #35C; font-weight: bold; letter-spacing: .5em; margin-bottom: 1em; text-transform: uppercase;)

You will note that the properties and their corresponding values are separated from other property/value pairs by using a semi-colon. You can opt to write the combine style rules as a single line similar to the example above or as multiple lines for better readability. The example below is just the same as Example 1:

Example 2:

h1 (

color: #35C;

font-weight: bold;

letter-spacing: .5em;

margin-bottom: 1em;

text-transform: uppercase;

)

How to Group Selectors

You can actually apply one single style to different selectors. All you really need to do is write all the selectors at the start of your style rule but make sure that they are separated by a comma. The examples above both pertain to the selector or property "level 1 heading". If you want to apply the same style rule to "level 2 heading" and "level 3 heading", you can include h2 and h3 in the first line, as follows:

Example:

```
h1, h2, h3 (

color: #35C;

font-weight: bold;

letter-spacing: .5em;

margin-bottom: 1em;

text-transform: uppercase;

)
```

Note that the sequence of the selector element is not relevant. You can write it as h3,h2,h1 and the style rule will exactly be the same. It means that the specified style rules will still be applied to all the elements of the selectors.

It is also possible to create a style rule that combines different class selectors.

Example:

```
#supplement, #footer, #content (

position: absolute;

left: 520px;

width: 210px;

)
```

Chapter 3: Methods of Associating Styles

There are actually 4 methods of associating styles within an HTML document – Embedded CSS, Inline CSS, External CSS and Imported CSS. But the two most frequently used are Inline CSS and External CSS.

Embedded CSS

This method uses the <style> element wherein the tags are positioned within the <head>...</head> tags. All elements that exist within your document will be affected by a rule that has been written using this syntax. The generic syntax is as follows:

<head>

<style type="text/css" media=". . .">

Style Rules

. . . .

</style>

</head>

The following attributes that are connected to the <style> element are as follows:

- Type with value "text/css". This attribute indicates the style sheet language as a content-type (MIME type). You need to note that this attribute is always required.

- Media with values as "screen", "tty", "tv", "projection", "handheld", "print", "braille", "aural" or "all". This attribute indicates what kind of device the webpage will be shown. This attribute is only optional and it always has "all" as a default value.

Example:

```
<head>

<style type="text/css" media="screen">

h2(

color: #38C;

)

</style>

</head>
```

Inline CSS

This method uses the style attribute of a specific HTML element in defining the style rule. This means that the style rule will only be applied to the specific HTML element ONLY. The generic syntax is as follows: <element style="...style rules....">

Only one attribute is connected to the <style> attribute and it is as follows:

- Style with value "style rules". The value that you will specify for the style attribute is basically a combination of various style declarations. You should use a semicolon to separate the different style declarations.

Example:

```
<h2 style ="color:#000;">. This is inline CSS </h2>
```

External CSS

This method uses the <link> element in defining the style rule. You can use it to add external style sheets within your webpage. The external style sheet that you will add will have a different text file that has the extension .css. All the style rules that you want to apply to your webpage elements will be added inside the external text file and then you can append the text file in any of your web pages by creating the <link> element. The general syntax that you will be using will be:

```
<head>

<link type="text/css" href=" . . ." media=" . . ." />

</head>
```

The following attributes that are connected with the <style> elements are as follows:

- Type with the value "text/css". This indicates that you are using a MIME type or a content type for your style sheet language. Note that you are always required to use this attribute.

- Href with value "URL". This attribute will indicate the specific style sheet file that contains your style rules. Again, you are also always required to use this attribute.

- Media with value "screen", "tty", "tv", "projection", "handheld", "print", "braille", "aural" or "all". This attribute indicates the specific media device that you will use to display the document. This attribute is only optional and it has a default value of "all".

Example wherein the style sheet file is named as docstyle.css:

```
h2, h3 (

color: #38C;

font-weight: bold;

letter-spacing: .5em;

margin-bottom: 2em;

text-transform: uppercase;

)
```

Then you can add your style sheet file "docstyle.css" in your webpage by adding these rules:

```
<head>
```

<link type="text/css" href="docstyle.css" media="all" />

</head>

Imported CSS

This method which uses the @import rule is the same as the <link> element because it is used to import an external style sheet file to your webpage. The generic syntax of this method is as follows:

<head>

<@import "URL";

</head>

Here is another alternative syntax that you can use:

<head>

<@import url ("URL");

</head>

Example:

<head>

@import "docstyle.css"'

</head>

How to Override CSS Style Rules

The following can override the style rules that you have created using the above four methods:

- An inline style sheet is given the number one priority. This means that an inline style sheet will always supersede a rule that has been written with a <style>...</style> tag or a rule that has been defined in an external stylesheet file.

- A rule that has been written with a <style>...</style> tag will always supersede a style rule that has been defined in an external stylesheet file.

- The rules that you define within an external stylesheet file is always given the lowest priority. This means that any rules defined within the external file will only be applied if the 2 rules above aren't valid.

How to Handle an Old Browser:

Currently, there are a lot of old browsers that are not yet capable of supporting CSS. When you are working with these kind of browsers, you need to write your embedded CSS within the HTML document. Here is an example on how you can embed CSS in an old browser:

```
<style type="text/css">

<!—

Body, td (

   Color: red;

)

-->

</style>
```

How to Add a CSS Comment

In case it is necessary for you to include an additional comment within the style sheet block, you can easily do this by writing your comment within /*....this is a comment in style sheet....*/. The /*....*/ method used in C++ and C programming languages can also be used in adding comments in a multi-line block.

Example:

```
/* This is an external style sheet file */

h3, h2, h1 (

color: #38C;

font-weight: bold;

letter-spacing: .5em;

margin-bottom: 2em;

text-transform: uppercase;

)

/* end of style rules. */
```

Chapter 4: Measurement Units

There are several measurements that CSS can support. These include absolute units like inch, centimeter, points, etc. They also include relative measures like em unit and percentage. These values are important when you want to specify the different measurements you want to include in your style rule. Example:

border="2px solid black".

Here are the most common measurements that you will use in creating CSS style rules:

Unit of Measure	Description	Example
%	Indicates measurements as a percentage in relation to another value which is normally an enclosing element	p {font-size: 12pt; line-height: 150%;}
cm	Indicates measurements in centimeter	div {margin-bottom: 1.5cm;}
em	A relative number used in measuring font height using em spaces. One em unit is equal to the size of a particular font. This means, if you want a certain font to have a size of 10pt, one "em" unit is equal to 10pt and 3em is equal to 30pt.	p {letter-spacing: 6em;}
ex	A number used to define a measurement in relation to the x-height of a font. The x-height is defined by the height of letter x in	p {font-size: 20pt: line-height: 2ex;}

	lowercase in any given font.	
in	Indicates measurements in inches	p {word-spacing: .12in;}
mm	Indicates measurements in millimeter	p {word-spacing: 12mm;}
pc	Indicates measurements in picas. One pica is equal to 12 points. This means that there are six picas in one inch.	p {font-size: 18pc;}
pt	Indicates measurements in points. One point is equal to 1/72 of one inch.	body {font-size: 20pt;}
px	Indicates measurements in screen pixel	p {padding: 32px;}

Chapter 5: Style Rules Using Colors

A color in CSS style rules is indicated by color values. Normally, the color values are used to define the color of either the background of an element or its foreground (that is, its text). You can also utilize colors to change how your borders and other aesthetic effects look.

Color values in CSS rules can be specified using the following formats:

- Hex code using the syntax #RRGGBB. Example: p {color: #FFFF00;}. The six digits represent one specific color wherein RR represents the value for red, GG the value for green and BB the value for blue. You can get the hexadecimal values of different colors from graphics software such as Jasc Paintshop Pro and Adobe Photoshop. You can also use the Advanced Paint Brush to get the hexadecimal values. You need to note that the six digits should always be preceded by the hash or pound sign (#).

- Short hex code using the syntax #RGB. Example: p {color: #7A6;}. This is the shorter version of the hexadecimal value. You can also get them from Jasc Paintshop Pro, Adobe Photoshop or Advanced Paint Brush.

- RGB % using the syntax rgb (rrr%, ggg%, bbb%). Example: p{color: rgb (40%, 50%, 40%);}. This format is actually advisable to use because not all browsers support this type of format.

- RGB Absolute using the syntax rgb (rrr,ggg, bbb). Example: p {color: rgb (255,0,0);}

- Keyword using the syntax black, aqua, etc. Example: p {color: red;}

Chapter 6: How to Set Backgrounds

What you will learn in this chapter includes how to define the background of the different elements in your web page. You can use any of the following background properties for specific elements in your webpage:

- You can use the background color property to define the background color of your element.

- You can use the background image property to define the background image of your element.

- You can use the background repeat property to control whether your background image will be repeated or not.

- You can use the background position property to control the position of the background image.

- You can use the background attachment property to define whether your image is fixed or will scroll with the rest of the webpage.

- You can use the background property to combine the above properties into one style rule.

Background Color

Here is a sample of how you can define the background color:

```
<p style=”background-color:red;”>

RED

</p>
```

This will result in RED.

Background Image

Here is a sample of how you can define the background image:

```
<table style=”background-image:url (/images/pattern1.jpg);”>

<tr><td>

The table now has an image in the background.

</td></tr>

</table>
```

How to Repeat a Background Image

In case your image is small, you can opt to repeat your background image. Otherwise, you can simple utilize the “no-repeat” value in the background-repeat property if you do not wish to have your background image repeated. This means that your image will only be displayed once. Note that “repeat value” is the default value in the background-repeat property.

Example:

```
<table style=”background-image:url (/images/pattern2.jpg);

              background-repeat: repeat;”>

<tr><td>

The background image in this table will be repeated several times.

</td></tr>

</table>
```

Here is a sample rule if you want the background image to be repeated vertically:

```
<table style=”background-image:url (/images/pattern2.jpg);
```

```
        background-repeat: repeat-y;">

<tr><td>

The background image in this table will be repeated vertically.

</td></tr>

</table>
```

Here is a sample rule if you want the background image to be repeated horizontally:

```
<table style="background-image:url (/images/pattern2.jpg);

        background-repeat: repeat-x;">

<tr><td>

The background image in this table will be repeated horizontally.

</td></tr>

</table>
```

How to Set the Position of the Background Image

Here is a sample of how you can define the position of a background image at 150 pixels from the left side:

```
<table style="background-image: url (/images/pattern2.jpg);

        Background-position:150px;">

<tr><td>

The position of the background is now 150 pixels from the left side.

</td></tr>
```

</table>

Here is a sample of how you can define the position of a background image at 300 pixels from the top and 150 pixels from the left side:

```
<table style="background-image: url (/images/pattern2.jpg);

                Background-position:150px 300px;">

<tr><td>

The position of the background is now 300 pixels from the top and 150 pixels from the left side.

</td></tr>

</table>
```

How to Define the Background Attachment

The background attachment indicates whether the background image that you have set is fixed in its place or scrolls when you move the webpage.

Here is an example on how to write a style rule with a background image that is fixed:

```
<p style="background-image:url (/images/pattern2.jpg);

                Background-attachment:fixed;">

The paragraph now has a background image that is fixed.

</p>
```

Here is an example on how to write a style rule with a background image that scrolls with the webpage:

```
<p style="background-image:url (/images/pattern2.jpg);

            Background-attachment:scroll;">

The paragraph now has a background image that scrolls with the webpage.

</p>
```

How to Use the Shorthand Property

You can actually utilize the background property in order to define all of the background properties all at the same time.

Example:

```
<p style="background:url (/images/pattern2.jpg) repeat scroll;">

The background image of this paragraph has a scroll and repeated properties.

</p>
```

Chapter 7: How to Set Font Properties

What you will learn in this chapter includes how to define the following font properties to a specific element in your webpage:

- You can use the font family property to adjust the face of your selected font.
- You can use the font style property to make your fonts either oblique or italic.
- You can use the font variant property to include the "small caps" effect in your fonts.
- You can use the font weight property to decrease or increase how light or bold your fonts are displayed.
- You can use the font size property to decrease or increase the sizes of your fonts.
- You can use the font property to define a combination of the font properties above.

How to Define the Font Family

Here is an example on how you can define the font family of a specific element. As value of the property, you can use any of the font family names available:

<p style="font-family:calibri,arial, serif;">

This message is displayed either in calibri, arial or the default serif font. It will depend on the existing fonts in your system.

</p>

How to Define the Font Style

Here is an example on how you can define the font style of a specific element. The values that you can use are oblique, italic or normal.

<p style="font-style:oblique;">

This message is displayed in oblique style.

</p>

How to Define the Font Variant

Here is an example on how you define the font variant of a specific element. The values that you can use are small-caps or normal.

<p style="font-variant:normal;">

This message is displayed in normal font variant.

</p>

How to Define the Font Weight

Here is an example on how you can define the font weight of a specific element. With this property, you will be able to define how bold you want your fonts to be. The values that you can use are bold, normal, lighter, bolder, 100, 200, 300, 400, 500, 600, 700, 800, and 900.

<p style="font-weight:normal;">

The font is displayed with normal font weight.

</p>

<p style="font-weight:lighter;">

The font is displayed with lighter font weight.

</p>

```
<p style="font-weight:800;">

The font is displayed with 800 font weight.

</p>
```

How to Define the Font Size

Here is an example on how you can define the font size of a specific element. With this property, you will be able to control the font sizes in your webpage. The values that you can use include small, medium, large, x-small, xx-small, xx-large, x-large, larger, smaller, size in % or size in pixels.

```
<p style="font-size:18px;">

The font is displayed with 18 pixels font size.

</p>

<p style="font-size:large;">

The font is displayed with large font size.

</p>

<p style="font-size:larger;">

The font is displayed with larger font size.

</p>
```

How to Define the Font Size Adjust

Here is an example on how you can define the font size adjust of a specific element. With this property, you will be able to adjust the x-height in order to make the legibility of your fonts better. The values that you can use include any number.

```
<p style="font-size-adjust:0.75;">
```

The font is displayed with 0.75 font size adjust value.

</p>

How to Define the Font Stretch

Here is an example on how you can define the font stretch of a specific element. With this property, you can allow the computer of your webpage readers to have a condensed or expanded version of the font you have defined in your elements. The values that you can use include normal, narrower, wider, condensed, extra-condensed, semi-condensed, ultra-condensed, semi-expanded, ultra-expanded, expanded and extra-expanded

<p style="font-stretch:ultra-condensed;">

If this does not seem to work, it is probably that the computer you are using does not have an expanded or condensed version of the font that was used.

</p>

How to Use the Shorthand Property

You can utilize the font property to define the font properties all at the same time.

Example:

<p style="font:oblique normal bolder 20px calibri;">

This applies all of the defined properties on the text all at the same time.

</p>

Conclusion

Thank you again for purchasing this book!

I hope this book was able to help you to understand the basic CSS styling rules.

The next step is to apply what you have just learned in your own webpage.

Finally, if you enjoyed this book, please take the time to share your thoughts and post a review on Amazon. We do our best to reach out to readers and provide the best value we can. Your positive review will help us achieve that. It'd be greatly appreciated!

Thank you and good luck!

Check Out My Other Books

Below you'll find some of my other popular books that are popular on Amazon and Kindle as well. Simply click on the links below to check them out. Alternatively, you can visit my author page on Amazon to see other work done by me.

Android Programming in a Day

Python Programming in a Day

C Programming Success in a Day

C Programming Professional Made Easy

JavaScript Programming Made Easy

PHP Programming Professional Made Easy

C ++ Programming Success in a Day

Windows 8 Tips for Beginners

Programming Box Set #29: C Programming Professional Made Easy & CSS Programming Professional Made Easy

HTML Professional Programming Made Easy

If the links do not work, for whatever reason, you can simply search for these titles on the Amazon website to find them.

www.ingramcontent.com/pod-product-compliance
Lightning Source LLC
Chambersburg PA
CBHW061034050326
40689CB00012B/2824
9781511755061